Just One Person

Charlotte Louise

BookLeaf Publishing
India | USA | UK

Just One Person © 2022 Charlotte Louise

All rights reserved.

No part of this publication may be reproduced, stored in a retrieval system, or transmitted, in any form or by any means, electronic, mechanical, photocopying, recording or otherwise, without the prior written permission of the presenters.

Charlotte Louise asserts the moral right to be identified as author of this work.

Presentation by *BookLeaf Publishing*

Web: www.bookleafpub.com

E-mail: info@bookleafpub.com

ISBN: **9789357446280**

First edition 2022

DEDICATION

To Colm, my future husband.

You keep me laughing, you keep me grounded,
but most of all, you keep me inspired.

PREFACE

I exist in a perpetual cycle of not recognising the person I was only a few months prior. However, I do not call this growth, I flash between Jekyll and Hyde, what one does, the other undoes. Growth, for me, feels like adding a link in the chain that ties me in place, widening the endless circle I tread.

The following collection of poetic journal entries explores the reality of living with Bipolar disorder. The way it can drastically shift your perspective back and forth can feel exhausting, but each side is still just one person, trying to exist between two planes, and trying to make it beautiful.

Half a Jar

I am half a jar of fireflies caught to keep myself
alight,
but this glass is lacking air holes and now my
chest feels tight.
I feel them burning up inside and soon they may
go out
if I can't learn to set them free and trust they'll
stick about.

I am half a jar of ocean that makes soothing
crashing sounds,
to fill my thoughts up with dreams of a distance
with no bounds.
But inside that jar, behind that glass, the distance
cannot spread,
no waves to carry thoughts off far, still waters in
my head.

The things I've tried to stay alive could kill me
in the end
and I can see that road ahead, it once felt like a
friend.
I need to turn around and walk the path I should
have chosen

but no matter what I fucking try, this jar won't fucking open.

13/03 - Enamoured

The lad at the counter in Tesco smiles, it reaches
his eyes, the palest of blues (sky) no, paler still,
the clouds in the sky, I soar through them,
disturb them, leave a tear through the center with
destructive fingers as I ascend above them. I
know that smile, electric. He tells me to have a
nice day, so I do.
I don't know his name, butterfly brain, I hunt for
a new face. I swipe endlessly, right, left, left,
left, right - a match, 2 miles away, let's go
dancing. A quick trip to Ann Summers,
overdraft looming, payday loans pay payday
loans, it doesn't matter, money is a man-made
concept; I am primal. I don't wait to get home,
trap my curves, my young body inside a pixel
monument, hit send - what if he leaks it? Good, I
look great.
We are at the club, music drums through my
chest, I follow it. Shots, shots, tinder guy goes to
the bar again, more drinks, shots, he goes again,
I find a new face while he's gone. We're back at
his place, I think. How? It doesn't matter, it's on.
Keep the party going; smoke this, sniff that, taste
him, skin to skin, euphoria.

The sky morphs in the distance; black, pink,
orange, blue. Shadows drift along the walls, I
drift out the door. Sleep eludes me, immortal, no
need for that, I skip home, a guy smiles at me
and I do it all again.

Bloom

5

Raindrops finally spill upon thirsty soil
after a long and heated summer.
The shadows on the window reflect
on skin like freckles, that trickle
down to the roots embedded fingertips.
Quench dry bones and bring them back.
Let roses bloom beneath the clattering ribcage
as petals blossom and thorns untangle inside.
Open now,
thriving,
alive once more.

Slow Fall

When I fell for you,
there were no scrapes
or fractures.
You took my hand
and guided me, slowly
to my knees and
pulled me into your arms.
Hammock,
you rock me
to and fro, the lullaby
of your heartbeat
soothes the chaos
behind my tired eyes.

13/09 - Enamoured

I lose myself. In the funhouse portal, I wince at the distorted reflection staring back. I write a novel in my head about all my broken parts that I'll never be able to fix, hills of flesh for miles, no man's land. Stretched marks of freshly turned soil with the goal to nurture any kind of growth, left barren and scared. Tulips wilting beneath my nose.

I pull away from the glass echo of myself. Curl up next to his strong body. Split mind: part of me longs for him to reach out and breath life in me. Roll up his sleeves and tend to my tattered weeds. The other part knows my land is too toxic, too dry, and dull for even the greenest thumb to graze. I close myself away, in a disused greenhouse with blacked-out windows. I bury myself deeper with each passing thought. Sprinkling more and more earth above me until I see no sunlight. Parched of affection.

As I lay beside him, I press against his body, try to awake the gardener in him. I feel for any kind of confirmation to prove I have the potential to grow, am I fertile? Despite myself, I slink around him like vines, clinging to his strong foundation. Climbing. I plant my last seed and wait for his next move; let me become tangled in overgrown misery, or water my self-deprecating thirst. He turns to the bedside table and takes out a pair of gardening gloves.

14/03 - Slumber

My jittery limps seek purpose, thoughts do laps,
and I chase them. Time feels finite and precious,
to rest is to waste, so I trap Sleep in a black satin
box where she cannot find me. But Nightmares
are impatient, they are smoke, they leak through
the keyhole - day or night, they still come.
Behind Sleep's back, the affair begins. We are
drawn to each other, moth, flame, I will be burnt
again, no visible scars, skin still searing as the
smoky figure pulls me close, we dance, a tango
between our two planes.
The first time they greeted me in consciousness
when the two realms merged, I feared them,
trapped in a cycle; nightmare, wake, paralysis,
wake, nightmare, wake again, I did not know
they followed me out of tortured slumber. I ran
to the door, heart pounding, ribcage straining, I
sought comfort from anyone nearby, Sing me a
lullaby, coo, like mothers do. I reached out for
the door but a misty hand reached back, I felt it
wrap around my wrist, I tore it back, became a
ball. WAKE UP, I willed the memory of its heat
coiled along my arm. Pinch, WAKE UP, pinch
through tears. I began to understand; Sleep had
left, I turned my back on her. Now only closed

eyes could shut out Nightmares, I made my bed
but could not lie in it.
Nightmares loomed, their infatuation grew,
stalking in every waking corner, reality bends -
one day I stalked back, made myself bigger,
louder than the bear, and a romance bloomed.

Spotlight

When that bright light hits
in the center of the stage,
headlights. My dear,
take a low bow.
It will be heavenly
to kick off those heels,
loosen the bra straps.
Take it all in
because you put on a
Damn. Good. Show.

Lullaby

Surrounded by life
void of people.
Natures sweet symphony
sways in the air.

Breeze whistles quietly,
soft tuneful chirps
harmonize with the
  splish
       splash
          splish
of the rippling lake.

Droplets of gold
light the sky
and warm the earth
with a loving embrace.

Sunlight sends tiny kisses
that flicker on the surface
where dances between
wind and water mesmerise.

14/09 - Slumber

The wailing alarm of my phone demands
consciousness. I come back, reluctantly from
that distant peaceful land and emerge from the
nest I made myself the night before. The sun
was still high and mighty in the sky when I last
closed my weary eyes. I've missed the sight of
stars for weeks. I squint at the harsh blue screen
that tells me it's time to live. A limitless list of
things to do and places to be, but the siren's
lullaby wills me to ignore them.
Today will be the day, I urge myself. But first,
five more minutes, I was dragged away from my
slumbering love before a kiss goodbye. I must
leave on kind terms, so the next encounter
remains sweet. I slide my finger across the
unforgiving glass. Snooze, and bury my head
under safety blankets, and fall deep into the arms
of Sleep once more. A comforting embrace, a
forgiving embrace. The goodbyes escape me
once more as I'm torn away, clinical, like a
doctor extracts a newborn; lungs retching as I
learn to grasp for air.
I start to slide my finger across the snooze
button once more, but my chilling heartaches to
thaw in Sleep's warm flame again. I turn off the

alarm, welcome the silence into my home, for as long as it's willing to stay with me. Delete the growing list of notifications. Olive branches cut. I inhale the familiar smell of unwashed hair and slide back into my stale cocoon.

15/03 - Reflection

I stare at a blank page, as deadlines creep towards me, responsibilities hang like a noose around my neck, rage builds in my chest. These rules should not apply to me, I am bigger than this. Weeks spent tending my own desires, now tied down to last-minute errands. Disconnect. I feel no attachment to these goals, to people - I have been dropped into a body that is not mine, It's spent so long tiptoeing around feelings, a ballerina with broken toenails. I shed its emotion like old skin, I burn memories I feel nothing for, roast marshmallows and get drunk, sing. Friends. Family. They search for that person I'm supposed to be, they need me to care, to give them everything again, but I've found the answer, and lead by example: do whatever the FUCK you want stop caring. I tread from whim to whim, It's all that grounds me, only feeling something when I get my way. Stop chasing me down with your problems, I have no other answers, I have no spare love left to give, It's all for me now, give me yours too, you're clearly not using it yourself.
Grandiose? It's a game I play with Karma, Tortoise, and the Hare (I know I'm faster).

Graceful, agile, fun, yet each time I make the
same mistake, get cocky, take a rest, lunch
break: Mock Turtle Soup. Before I know it,
Karma creeps across the finish line, I'm
banished to my rabbit hole. Buried.

Coventry

I get nostalgic thinking about coffee shops,
despite never drinking a cup in my life.
After long trips on young legs
wandering through a maze of silks and cotton,
We fall into the comfort of that strong smell
and order hot chocolate, pretending
to be more grown-up than we were.

We'd empty the contents of new bags,
new notebooks and coloured pens,
delicate fingers grasping their potential.
We'd brand our names in the margin
and the background chatter fades,
leaving only your childlike laugh
syncopated with the beating of young hearts.

Although we've grown up,
there's no need to grow out
of the little things that made life
feel incredible for a few moments.
I get nostalgic thinking about coffee shops
and find myself making cups I know
I won't drink.

My Father's First Gift

Not the last name
given to him
and to myself by chance,
but the first name
gave to me
by choice.

"You will continue a legacy,
hold great grandma's hand
and both bow
when the name is called.
Carry her with you
in all that you do."

"There will be French in you,
another tongue to wrap
around new words.
Another mind to play in
and another place
to call home."

"You will be a strong woman,

and can never lose that
no matter how often you are
called from another mouth.
You will be reminded each time
You sign part of your life away."

"You will have a choice,
a name that can be molded
to fit your ever-changing moods,
ever-growing personality.
I will name you
with very few limits."

The first gift he gave to me
will not die with me.
It is found at the end
of each lifeline I write,
in the corner of every choice
I paint on my canvas.

He gave me the mark
I will leave on this earth.
Sharing it is my privilege.

-Charlotte, Charlie, Chaz, Charles, Lottie,
Tottie… Princess

15/09 - Reflection

My legs, too weak to carry the burden of myself, buckle. Each step pulls me closer and closer to the ground. Finally, I let myself drop. Crumble. Shards skid out in every direction, not for the first time. I ache, tired of picking up my own pieces time after time. I've begun to hand them out, to ease the heavy load I bear. Cut them to size, file the edges down and leave a pile of dust that was once part of me, stirring in the cold breeze. I whittle them down so they can patch the empty spaces of those around me. I'd rather be useful than whole.
I breathe air from my own lungs into winded soldiers and pull them off the ground. Let them stand on my shoulders, squint for a glimpse of hope in the distance. I lay across the ocean, a body to step across, I'll keep their feet dry and guide them to the other side. I'll emerge dripping, throw my hair back – Little Mermaid – and give them my voice. Teach them to ask for what they want. I'll give them that too.
Whatever it is.
My purpose will be to give purpose. As long as I have that, and only with that, will I feel worthy to take up this space? It is a selfish need, to be

needed. I live in fear of my last day that goes away. When I've handed out the last of my pieces and disappear completely.

16/03 - Devastation

For just a moment, I catch myself losing steam, exhaustion creeps, euphoria is slipping. I do whatever it takes to keep that feeling going, ride that train off the tracks, I stand on a small ledge in a high place, get my heart racing, chasing adrenaline. But my breathing stays calm, can I even die, I don't feel like I can? I push my body's limits, fill my lungs, my veins with poisons that mimic mania. I take a kitchen knife, glide it along a honing steel, skin prickling at the sound of scraping metal, hairs raising in response. Poised. Ready. I take the blade and drag it along my skin. Just to see if I can bleed. Ignore the red river that runs down to my fingertips. Fake news. I feel fine, untouchable. Pay no mind to concerned coos of friends cursed with mortality - take a torch to the bridges, it's better that way, isn't it? Martyr myself, lone wolf; spare them the pain of believing I can destroy myself. I'll never come down. Give me an army of Yes men, enablers. Trust in me. In what I want. I'm a master of rhetoric. Dictator. Monarch. But I can already see the future. A continuous cycle. One day they will revolt.

Hide. Move on, start fresh. Build again. Repeat.
I like roundabouts. Spin faster, feel the weight of
gravity pull me to the floor. The icy whip of
wind on my cheeks. Air crystallising in my
lungs. I can go around, and around. That's just
fine.

Concrete Jungle

If this is the concrete jungle
does that make us animals?

Thunderous roaring traffic,
vicious howling winds
that whip between
brick mountains.

Busy lives swarm
from place to place.
Clockwork instincts,
greedy creatures of habit.

Life becomes a battle,
survival of the fittest;
unnatural selection.
Unseeing eyes always win.

Some beg, others thrive,
prey upon the weak – the kind.
All look out for number one,
ignoring Mother Nature's plea.

We are not animals,
we are worse than that

we lack peace and harmony.
We are human.

Inevitable

Sleep away the sunny hours,
toss and turn in the dark.
Stare for hours at
what could have been
a perfectly alabaster-white ceiling,
if it weren't for that
damn smudge.
Why is self-destruction so
imminent?
Why does evil feel so
heavenly?
Would you risk
eternal damnation,
for the crisp crunch of an apple
on a muggy summer's day?
Is it worth the effort
to keep making the right choices,
is perfection really necessary?
Because all I can think about
is how boring the ceiling would be
to stare at without that
damn smudge.

16/09 - Devastation

The air becomes sparse, I must ration my breathing. I feel myself suffocating under expectation, from a time where I thought I could handle more than any human could. I sought comfort in isolation, show no weakness. I did not burn my bridges, it's just been so long since I've traveled them, I don't remember how to get to them. The scarcely trodden paths that led me to them are now overgrown with weeds and wildflowers. What right do I have anyway, to stomp through their home for my benefit? Just to cross a bridge that nobody wants me to. I imagine their stone, beaten down by salty air, moss growing in crevices, the chinks in its armour. The feeling mirrors in me; the moment I start to falter, lose steam, doubt plunges itself inside and spreads through the cracks in my façade.

It becomes a self-fulfilling prophecy – you can't if you think you can't – I repeat the backward mantra in my head until my very foundations crumble. Now here I lie, a dog-pile of responsibilities and an ever-shrinking timeframe. I've let myself become crippled by the fear of letting anyone down. Allowing them to move their own furniture into my walls. Small at first, a toothbrush, shampoo, it wasn't enough, I had to make them feel at home, despite knowing it would topple down. I was built on soft soil. I've been sinking from the moment I was made. A leaning eyesore that locals petition to demolish. I'd sign in a heartbeat if anyone cared to ask.

17/03 - Resilience

I turn the tap. Inspiration gushes through. I cup my hands underneath and catch whatever falls. Raise it to my pale lips and quench my thirst after a dull, hot summer. Splash my dry skin. Revitalise. Let it cascade down my hair, along the contours of my back, my hips, to my toes. Cool the burning desire, inflamed beneath my skin. The need to create. Ideas start to pool. I watch a bead escape and trickle in its own direction. I follow. Become fluid. Another drop speeds past, catching my eye. Bigger. Faster. I chase it. Freeze it. Chip away and build a sculpture in my own image. Heat it. Dance in the steam.

Behind me, a lake of potential begins to spread, far, wide, deep. I kick my shoes off. Take the first step into its warm embrace. I feel brave. Take risks. Deep breath, I baptise myself. Drift in the womb of opportunity. Reborn. Serenaded by the metallic tinkle below the water's surface. Allow the current to guide me in my next direction. I stretch out and feel the ground beneath me once more. Land ho! Wade back to shore. Feel a sunny breeze start to dry my skin as I stare at the fresh canvas I was delivered to. I wipe the sand from my feet with a blank page and frame it. The water begins to drain from my ears. Squeaky-clean mind. I take a stick to the wet ground and draw blueprints. Build a new home where inspiration dropped me.

Balancing Act

Sanity
is a taught tightrope
too thin spread
to tiptoe along.
It is etched
in the walls of closed minds
to naturally lean
in either direction
and plummet.
There is a stigma
behind safety nets,
in hope that each bone
broken, is a reminder
to stay within the limits.
But we're too stiff
to be acrobats.
Too clumsy
to be dancers.
Too big
to gracefully walk
the fine line,
so maybe we'll
learn to swing.

17/09 - Resilience

I was a rainbow once, a twisting pattern of light slicing through an open sky. Mothers taught their children to believe I was led to all kinds of treasures. Now, I've become a pallet of the night sky; black and blue mostly. From time to time, I'm doused in red, though that fades to a purple-grey, painted in scars from the constant battle against myself. I count them off in pride. A tally on my skin of all the times I've been knocked down and got back up again. I've learnt to be agile, to duck and dive from the blows and punch back harder. Study each fight. Know what comes next, strategise and recover. When the bell rings and I have time to breathe, I savour each inhale deeply. Step back and compose myself when it gets too fast. Self-nurture becomes second nature.

One day, in the not so distant future, I'll return to my multi-coloured state; understand every hue of emotion there is. I will be rewarded with unending empathy. That is the pot of gold the mothers told us all about. On that day, I'll be able to hang up my gloves. Ringside, stand tall with pride. Extend my hand towards other beaten-down souls and teach them how I became

a winner. Ice their aching muscles and cheer
them on from the crowd, until they too can
shake their own hand in acceptance and retire
from the fight.

I'm Fine
(Continued)*

"I'm fine"

Blood veins, now overgrown dirt paths
forgot, no longer traveled.
New journeys spread out ahead,
still uncertain where they will lead,
it's not impossible to learn
how to handle wolves in dark caves.
Tame with love.
Take off the ear to ear mask,
let them see your naked face,
love that too.
In that freedom, you will learn
how it feels to really smile.

"I'm really fine"

Become a master
of jigsaw puzzles.
It's more fun to ignore
the picture on the box.
Stick pieces together that don't match

but still fit, hand in hand.
Hold your own hand,
thank your unsteady legs
for the burdens they've carried
and show them how it feels
to run and skip.
Let breeze pull you forward like strings.

"I'm honestly fine"

The pounding of your heart
shook rabbit holes.
Caving in around you,
but you were not buried
beneath the earth.
It opened up and cradled you,
in an embrace of dirt and grass,
Finally, rest your weary head.
The cage doors aren't just open,
they're broken beyond repair.
But broken isn't always bad.

You said
"I'll be fine"
and today
It's time to believe it.

*A response to 'I'm Fine' from "The Little Book of Lies" collection